PEARL HARBOR
and the
USS ARIZ MEMORIAL:
A PICTORIAL HISTORY*

Written, Compiled and Edited by:

Richard A. Wisniewski

Designed and Arranged by:

Herbert Goeas

Printed in Honolulu, Hawaii by:

Pacific Printers, Inc.

•

Published and Distributed by:

Pacific Basin Enterprises
P.O. Box 8924
Honolulu, Hawaii 96815

TABLE OF CONTENTS

Dedicated to the entire membership of the Fleet Reserve Association. Working with Pearl Harbor-Honolulu Branch 46, the Fleet Reserve Association has, since 1964, continually strived to make improvements to the USS Arizona Memorial and the visitor accommodations at the memorial landing. The membership of the entire association feels very strongly that Pearl Harbor is a cherished part of our naval heritage.

PEARL HARBOR PRIOR TO DECEMBER 7, 1941

Unidentified U. S. warship in Honolulu harbor sometime in the late 1890's. When Captain Cook discovered the Hawaiian Islands in 1778, Pearl Harbor was known as "Wai Momi," meaning "water of pearl." Its name grew out of the pearl oysters that were found in its waters. Pearl divers believed that a benevolent shark goddess protected the waters. Because a coral bar blocked the entrance, Pearl Harbor was not considered a suitable port site in those early days. **State Archives**

The *Charleston* in Honolulu harbor, January 29, 1891. King David Kalakaua, suffering from ill health, sailed on the *Charleston* in hopes of improving his health in California. Unfortunately, he died there and his remains were returned to Hawaii aboard the *Charleston*. **State Archives**

Early photo of the *USS Boston* (left) and other ships in Honolulu's harbor about 1898. In 1840, an observant Navy Lieutenant named Charles Wilkes, while surveying the Pearl Harbor estuary, calculated that the obstructing coral could be blasted away to allow deep draft ships to enter the harbor. The Spanish-American War confirmed the strategic value of Pearl Harbor as an advance base, but many more years would pass before the actual dredging took place. **State Archives**

Rear Admiral Corwin P. Reese and staff at the hoisting of the Admiral's flag at the Honolulu Naval Station near the Honolulu waterfront (1909). The U. S. Navy's first contact with Hawaii came in 1826 when the *USS Dolphin*, a schooner, visited the Islands. In May of 1899, the Naval Coal Depot at Honolulu (later renamed Naval Station) was commissioned and construction began on two piers. Expansion continued and in 1911, *USS California* (Armored Cruiser 6) became the first large ship to enter the dredged channel and anchor off the Naval Station. In 1913, the Admiral and his staff moved to a new administration building at Pearl Harbor. The Marines, who arrived in 1903, moved to Pearl Harbor in 1914. **State Archives**

A cartoon by R. Yardley depicting an eager Uncle Sam surveying a map of Pearl Harbor and attempting to decide on how best to spend the more than $10,000,000 appropriated by the Congress in the early 1900's. By 1921, the Navy had spent more than $40,000,000 in Hawaii, nearly all of it at Pearl Harbor. **State Archives**

Pearl Harbor in 1908. The United States obtained exclusive rights to Pearl Harbor in 1884 after a long period of negotiations with the Hawaiian monarchy. In exchange, Congress allowed Hawaiian sugar to enter the United States duty free. The coral bar which blocked the entrance to the harbor was dredged to a depth of 35 feet in 1902, thereby allowing deep draft vessels to enter. **Official Navy Photo**

Initial work involved dredging the channel, building work shops and constructing a dry dock. **State Archives**

Collapsed dry dock (February 18, 1913). Work on the first dry dock at Pearl Harbor began in October of 1909. Many natives in the vicinity were horrified because according to legend, there once were coral caves on the site in which the great Shark God of the South Seas lived. Nonetheless, work progressed. Two attempts to empty the dry dock were unsuccessful and additional work had to be performed. On the third attempt, the dry dock collapsed in the afternoon of February 17th. The Shark God was angered said the natives. Seismic disturbance countered the engineers. **Official Navy Photo**

The submarine *F-1* (SS-20) operating in Hawaiian waters about 1914. Her Flotilla was the first to be based in Honolulu. Between July 21, 1914 and November 14, 1915, the Flotilla conducted development operations in the Hawaiian Islands. The Submarine Base at Pearl Harbor was later established in 1920. **Official Navy Photo**

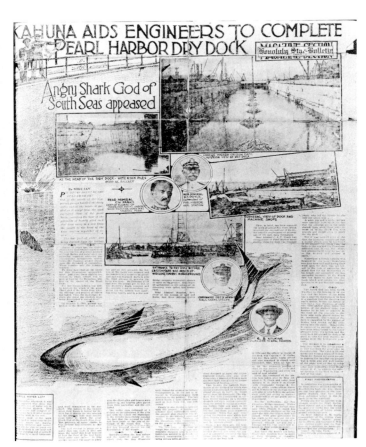

Article which appeared in the April 5, 1919 edition of the Honolulu Star-Bulletin. **Honolulu Star-Bulletin/Navy Photo**

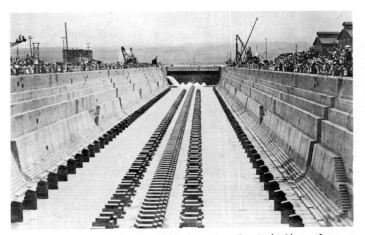

Formal opening of the Pearl Harbor Dry Dock (#1) on August 21, 1919. After the first failure, work started again in December of 1914. Top engineers were consulted and a new method was devised. In the meantime, a female kahuna was summoned by the Hawaiians to appease the angry Shark God. This time, the dry dock held. According to the engineers, the 16 feet of concrete (twice the previous amount) at the bottom of the basin plus other modern engineering features assured the success of the dry dock. **Official Navy Photo**

Birds-eye view of the Naval Station coaling plant at Pearl Harbor taken from radio tower #1 August 18, 1919.
Official Navy Photo

Pearl Harbor — July 8, 1920. Panoramic view of the yard and drydock #1 looking east. To the left are the battleships *Michigan* and *South Carolina* at 1010 wharf and the *Kansas* moored at buoy #3. **Official Navy Photo**

The Pearl Harbor Naval Hospital at Hospital Point in 1921.
Official Navy Photo

An Army PN-9 flying boat towing two surfing enthusiasts off Ford Island in August, 1922. Note that the "surfers" are hanging on to the tow lines. **State Archives**

The Submarine Base at Pearl Harbor in April of 1925.
Official Navy Photo

Aerial view of the seaplane station at the southern tip of Ford Island (March 5, 1926). **Official Navy Photo**

A December 12, 1930 view of the Submarine Base at Pearl Harbor showing submarine divisions 9 & 14. **Official Navy Photo**

The Pearl Harbor industrial complex as it appeared in 1934.
Official Navy Photo

The Pearl Harbor main gate as it looked in March of 1934.
Official Navy Photo

PAN AM's Sikorsky survey flight cruises past Diamond Head in this picture taken in April, 1935. This flight blazed the trail for the "China Clipper's" arrival later in November, opening up the Pacific to air travel.

PAN AM Photo/Kamaaina Graphics Collection

April 17, 1935. The Pan American Clipper stops at the Naval Air Station, Ford Island Seaplane Base enroute to Manila. This base was used on a regular basis from October, 1936 through early 1940.
Official Navy Photo

Duke Kahanamoku (extreme left in front of microphone) hosts Hawaii's welcoming ceremony at Pearl Harbor for the crew of Pan Am's "China Clipper." The pilot is Captain Edwin Musick (third from right). Governor Joseph Poindexter (second from right) looks on.

PAN AM Photo/Kamaaina Graphics Collection

The Pearl Harbor Naval Shipyard undergoing expansion in 1936.
Official Navy Photo

The shipyard after completion in 1938.   **Official Navy Photo**

USS Honolulu arrives in Honolulu at pier 2 on July 9, 1939, prior to taking up her first duty station at Pearl Harbor. *Honolulu,* a light cruiser (CL-48), was officially commissioned on June 15, 1938 with Captain Oscar Smith in command. Her total construction cost was in excess of $15,000,000.

Official Navy Photo

In the welcoming ceremony, a sterling silver punchbowl set styled after a Hawaiian calabash was presented to the *Honolulu* by the people of the city and county of Honolulu. She acquired the nickname "Blue Goose" because of the blue seaplane she carried and the blue coat of paint she wore when serving as flagship for the admiral and his staff. The ship's motto was "Lanakila Mau" (always victorious). **Official Navy Photo**

USS Saratoga (CV-3) and *USS Lexington* (CV-2) at anchor off Diamond Head prior to the outbreak of war. As the United States moved closer to war in the Atlantic, Pacific Fleet ships were transferred to the Atlantic Fleet. This left only three carriers in the Pacific — *Saratoga, Lexington* and *Enterprise* (CV-6). On the morning of December 7th, the Japanese found no carriers in port. Fortunately for the United States, *Saratoga* was on the West Coast, *Lexington* was scheduled to arrive at Midway with a squadron of Marine scout bombers, and *Enterprise,* operating under war-time conditions due to deteriorating Japanese-American relations, was returning from delivering Marine fighter planes to Wake Island. *Enterprise* was scheduled to arrive in Pearl Harbor on Saturday December 6th, but heavy seas had slowed down the task force. **Official Navy Photo**

The carrier *USS Enterprise* (CV-6) enroute to Pearl Harbor.
National Archives

Rear Admiral Chester Nimitz (at microphone) being relieved by Rear Admiral Russel Willson (right) as Commander, Battleship Division one, on board the *USS Arizona* at San Pedro, California (May, 1939). Admiral Nimitz went to Washinton to become Chief of the Bureau of Navigation. The skipper of the *Arizona*, Captain Isaac Kidd, later was promoted to Rear Admiral and held the same command as his predecessors aboard the *Arizona*. He was killed when *Arizona* was attacked on December 7, 1941.
Official Navy Photo

Units of the U. S. Pacific Fleet anchored off Pearl Harbor in 1940. **Official Navy Photo**

Aerial view of Ford Island taken January 30, 1941. "Battleship Row" is on the right. **Official Navy Photo**

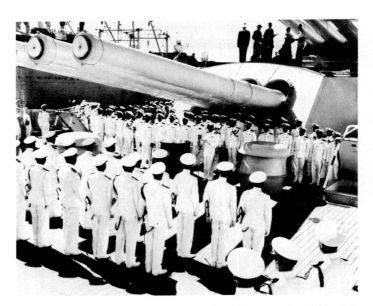

Pacific Fleet change of command. On February 1, 1941, Admiral Husband E. Kimmel relieved Admiral James O. Richardson in ceremonies aboard the flagship *USS Pennsylvania*. On the same day, the United States Fleet (with a Battle Fleet in the Pacific and a Scouting Fleet in the Atlantic) was reorganized into separate Atlantic and Pacific Fleets. The shore headquarters for the Pacific Fleet was established at Pearl Harbor.
Official Navy Photo

USS ARIZONA (BB-39)

The beginning of a legend. The *Arizona* being launched at the New York Navy Yard (1915). **Shipmate "Pappy" Frazier Photo**

Tugs gently ease the flag-covered *Arizona* alongside the pier after her launching on June 19, 1915 under the sponsorship of Miss Esther Ross, daughter of W.W. Ross, a prominent pioneer citizen of Prescott, Arizona. *Arizona* was commissioned on October 17, 1916 with Captain John D. McDonald, USN, in command. **Official Navy Photo**

USS Arizona departing New York, 1918. She was a unit of the honor escort that brought President Woodrow Wilson into Brest, France, on December 13th for the Paris Peace Conference. **Official Navy Photo**

Mightiest ship of the fleet in the 1920's, the 608 ft. Arizona had cage masts and side-mounted guns. The white-faced, 10 numbered range clock on the mainmast told her gunners the distance of targets. In this picture, the 31,000-ton Arizona rides at anchor.
Official Navy Photo

The USS Arizona (BB-39) in all her glory with all guns trimmed fore-and-aft. Note the crew turned out in blues and pea jackets. This photo was taken sometime in the early 1930's after she completed her modernization overhaul in Norfolk, Va. Arizona's cage masts were replaced with tripod-type masts, and new five-inch guns replaced her old three-inch anti-aircraft battery. In addition, she received increased horizontal armor for protection from high-angle gunfire and aircraft bombs. Additional outer plating in defense of torpedoes or underwater bombs was also added. To offset the extra weight, Arizona received new boilers and new main cruising turbines which enabled her to maintain her normal fleet speed of 16.8 knots. **Official Navy Photo**

USS Arizona in drydock at the Navy Yard, Pearl Harbor, March 2, 1932. Assigned to Battleship Division Three, Battle Force, *Arizona* spent the remainder of her career in the Pacific. Based at San Pedro, her cruising grounds extended south to Panama, north to Seattle and west to Hawaii. **Official Navy Photo**

All ahead full, *Arizona* cuts a wide path through rough water as she "steams from San Pedro to San Francisco," according to an undated note written on the back of this picture. On April 2, 1940, *Arizona* departed San Pedro to her new base at Pearl Harbor. At the end of September, she returned to the west coast for an overhaul. On January 23, 1941, Rear Admiral Isaac C. Kidd relieved Admiral Willson on board *Arizona* as Commander, Battleship Division One. She returned to Pearl Harbor on February 3 for intensive battle readiness maneuvers and returned again to the west coast in June. **Official Navy Photo**

USS Arizona entering Pearl Harbor. Returning from the west coast, she arrived in Pearl Harbor on July 8th. Her future destiny, less than five months away, was already being planned by the Japanese. **Official Navy Photo**

"OPERATION HAWAII"- THE JAPANESE ATTACK

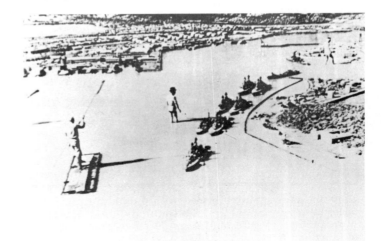

The air attack on Pearl Harbor was conceived by Admiral Isoruku Yamamoto, Commander-in-Chief of the Japanese Combined Fleet. Having served as a naval attache in Washington from 1925 to 1927, Yamamoto knew American ways, her industrial potential and the manner in which Americans could and would fight if aroused. Although initially opposed to war with the United States, he resigned himself to war under pressure from the Army-ruled Japanese government and its expansionist plans. He thus became a strong proponent of the attack on Pearl Harbor. The purpose of the attack was to sink or cripple large units of the Pacific Fleet so that they would not interfere with Japan's southern thrust toward the Philippines and especially the East Indies with its strategic supplies of oil, rubber and other commodities. Denied oil by the United States, Japan needed an alternate source for her undeclared war with China.

Official Navy Photo

The Japanese planning the Pearl Harbor attack. In April of 1941, a carrier air attack study had been completed. During the summer, the Japanese Fleet held maneuvers for its carrier planes. In September, the plan to strike Hawaii was approved, although no date was set. In November, just one month before the raid, final approval was given and the date of December 7th was tentatively selected. On December 2nd, the final date for the attack was announced. Because the 7th was a Sunday, it was felt by the Japanese Naval General Staff that surprise could be achieved and that a majority of the Hawaii-based ships would be in port for the weekend, as had been the custom.

Official Navy Photo

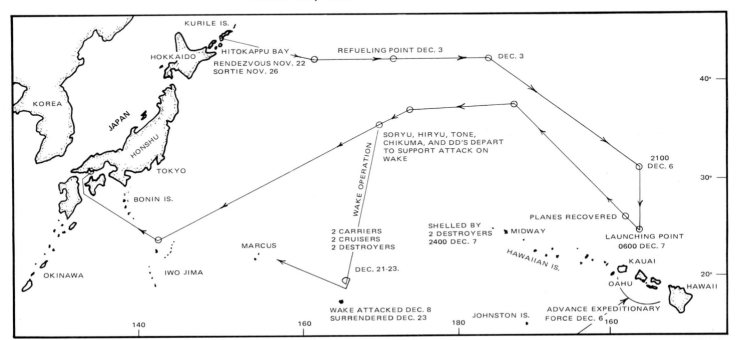

Commanded by Vice Admiral Chuichi Nagumo, the attack force assembled in Hitokappu Bay in the remote Kuril Islands. Arriving in small numbers, maximum secrecy was observed. On November 26, the attack force sailed on a northern route to avoid detection by other ships and aircraft. Despite the anticipated bad weather, the northern route would greatly increase the chances for complete surprise. High seas, gales and dense fog washed men overboard, ripped signal flags and threatened collisions during refueling. Nevertheless, the attack force proceeded on schedule, encountering only one ship — a Japanese freighter.

Diagram compiled from official sources

COMPOSITION OF THE JAPANESE ATTACK FORCE

AIR ATTACK FORCE
SIX CARRIERS
Akagi
Kaga
Hiryu
Soryu
Shokaku
Zuikaku

SUPPORT FORCE
2 BATTLESHIPS
2 HEAVY CRUISERS

SCREENING FORCE
1 LIGHT CRUISER
9 DESTROYERS

PATROL FORCE
3 SUBMARINES ("I" type)

SUPPLY FORCE
8 OILERS

Since the warships were loaded with drums of extra fuel, the oilers returned to Japan on December 3rd after refueling the ships. An additional twenty-seven fleet submarines were to deploy around Oahu to torpedo any U.S. warships which might try to escape. The "I" type submarines carried a two-man midget submarine "piggyback" style. They would attempt to penetrate the harbor and add to the chaos.

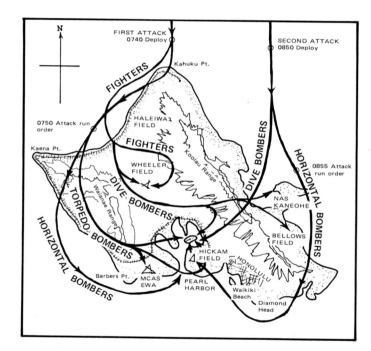

A Japanese "Kate" torpedo-bomber prepares to take off from the carrier Soryu as Japanese sailors give a "Banzai" salute.
Official Navy Photo

At 6:00 A.M. on December 7th, the first wave of 183 planes began taking off from the six carriers stationed about 200 miles due north of Oahu. They consisted of torpedo-bombers, high-level bombers, dive-bombers and fighters. Upon sighting the Oahu coastline at about 7:40 A.M., they deployed: the fighters to gain control of the air and destroy parked planes at Wheeler and Kaneohe; the high-level bombers for Hickam Field; the dive-bombers for Wheeler Field and the Naval Air Station at Ford Island; and the torpedo-bombers for the battleships and cruisers. Since the battleships were mostly docked in pairs, the torpedo-bombers concentrated on the outboard ships while the horizontal-bombers concentrated on the inboard battleships using 1760-pound armor-piercing bombs.

The second wave of attack planes was launched an hour and fifteen minutes later. This wave consisted of approximately 170 planes. The fighters' mission was to meet any airborne resistance or strafe the airfields. The horizontal-bombers concentrated on Hickam Field while the dive-bombers again aimed for the major ships of the Pacific Fleet.

Diagram compiled from official sources

Japanese propaganda leaflet. The Japanese translation is "Hear! The voice of the moment of death. Wake up, you fools." Each aviator had a map detailing the exact location of his target. Since no aircraft carriers were in port, these fliers attacked the battleships and the *Utah* which apparently looked like a carrier from the air, but actually was a former battleship converted into a target ship.   **Official Navy Photo**

Captured photo showing the Japanese pilots view as they approached Pearl Harbor on Sunday morning. Ford Island is in the center and "Battleship Row" is on the eastern side of the island. The Naval Shipyard is on the far right. Bomb splashes can be seen as the attack is already underway. Just prior to the taking of this picture, Commander Mitsuo Fuchida, in command of the first wave, transmitted a coded message indicating that the attack was a surprise — "Tora . . . Tora . . . Tora" ("Tiger . . . Tiger . . . Tiger").   **Official Navy Photo**

The hospital ship *USS Solace* (AH-5) photographed from a motor launch on December 7th just as the first wave of attacking Japanese planes came out of the protective cloud cover above the Waianae Mountain Range. The tiny dark spots in the lighter clouds midway between the ship's stack and rear mast are the attackers spotted by members of the crew gathered on the fantail awaiting morning colors and the first liberty launch ashore. With her hull painted white and with large red crosses on both sides as well as topside, the attackers did not bomb or strafe the *Solace*. The *Solace* joined the Pacific Fleet on October 7, 1941, Navy Day, and received her first baptism to combat just two months later. Lifeboats from the *Solace* quickly sprang in action picking up the wounded and returning them to the ship for treatment. One of the first small boats to reach the capsized *Oklahoma* was a lifeboat from the *Solace*.

Ralph Morse/Time (Life) Inc.
with special permission through the courtesy of
Ens. H.C. "Pat" Daly, MSC, USN-Retired.

"Battleship Row" under attack. At the bottom, left, is the *Nevada;* then the *Arizona* with the repair ship *Vestal* outboard; the *Tennessee* and the *West Virginia* (outboard and already sinking); the *Maryland* and the *Oklahoma* (outboard); and the oiler *Neosho.* Hickam Field, in the background, is already under attack. **Official Navy Photo**

Dive-bomber's view of "Battleship Row."   **Official Navy Photo**

Ford Island hangars burning during the attack. The first enemy bombs struck Ford Island at 7:55 A.M. Within a matter of minutes, all fighting planes were destroyed or damaged prior to the torpedo attacks against the ships. The airfields at Hickam, Wheeler, Ewa, Bellows and Kaneohe were also bombed and strafed with machine gun fire, thereby eliminating any major aerial threat to the attacking planes.   **Official Navy Photo**

Wheeler Field under attack. Here as at Hickam Field, the planes were lined up in neat rows with only ten feet between wing-tips. This anti-sabotage measure proved extremely costly; for as soon as one plane was hit, it became a fountain of fire, spreading its flames to the next plane. **Army Signal Corps/Hickam AFB**

Hickam Field under attack. About 7:00 A.M., an Army radar operator at a remote mobile search radar station on Oahu's northern point, picked up an enormous flight of planes. However, two ironic twists of fate caused this flight of planes to be ignored. First, the radar station was used to train operators and it was operated only on Sunday from 4:00 A.M. to 7:00 A.M. Second, a widely publicized flight of B-17 bombers was expected to arrive that morning.   **Army Signal Corps/Hickam AFB**

Smoke billows from the flight line at Hickam Field. In the midst of the attack, about 12 Army B-17 bombers arrived. To make the long flight from California, their guns were coated with cosmoline and they carried no ammunition. They were attacked, but all managed to land at various bases on Oahu. One even landed on a golf course. *

Another group of scout bombers from the carrier *Enterprise* arrived a short time later. Out-gunned and out-maneuvered, eleven of the total of 18 managed to land on Ford Island's battered runway.   **Army Signal Corps/Hickam AFB**

Fire-fighting teams attempting to save a stricken plane at Kaneohe.   **Navy Photo/Kaneohe MCAS**

Kaneohe Naval Air Station under attack.
Navy Photo/Kaneohe MCAS

A "Val" dive-bomber preparing to attack. **Official Navy Photo**

A sailor stationed on Ford Island in the center of Pearl Harbor watches as the battleship *Arizona* explodes. To his right is the burned-out wing of a PBY Catalina. A number of single-engine scout planes survived the holocaust. **Official Navy Photo**

Within one minute after the Japanese attack commenced, the *USS Arizona* was shattered by torpedo and bomb explosions. One armor-piercing bomb penetrated *Arizona's* forward powder magazine. The resulting explosion wrecked half the battleship and killed her commanding officer, Captain Franklin Van Valkenburgh, and Rear Admiral Kidd, both on the bridge at the time. This tremendous blast caused *Arizona* to sink in nine minutes, so fast that hundreds of men were trapped below. Of the 1177 Officers and enlisted men killed, 75 bodies were recovered and the remaining 1102 are still entombed in the sunken battleship. **Official Navy Photo**

USS California, struck by two torpedoes and one bomb, struggles to stay afloat. The ship sank over a period of three days because her manholes and ventilation systems were open and pipelines had ruptured. In addition, an oil fire from the burning *Arizona* caused the ship to be temporarily abandoned. Intentional counterflooding was resorted to in order to prevent the ship from capsizing as the *Oklahoma* had done. **Official Navy Photo**

USS Shaw's (DD-373) forward magazines blew up in a spectacular explosion. Being in an overhaul status in Floating Drydock Number Two, Shaw's ammunition was stowed below and she could not open fire on her attackers. She was hit by three bombs from the same dive-bombers that attacked the Nevada. The first two penetrated the forecastle and the main decks and were in part responsible for severing her bow forward of the bridge. The third bomb ruptured Shaw's fuel oil tanks, spreading burning oil throughout the forward portion of the ship. The intense heat from this fire triggered the explosion.

Official Navy Photo

USS Nevada aground and on fire. Moored by herself, Nevada managed to get underway despite flooding caused by a plane-launched torpedo and several bomb hits. Moving toward the main channel, a flight of Japanese bombers spotted her and concentrated their attacks on her. Enemy bombs caused huge geysers to form around the ship. Still underway, Nevada emerged, her superstructure on fire and her hull a series of gaping holes. Fearing she might sink and block the channel, two tugs were ordered to assist her. They pushed Nevada clear of the channel and beached her at Waipio Point, opposite the southern end of Ford Island. There, the fires were brought under control.

Official Navy Photo

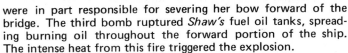

USS West Virginia resting on the bottom of the harbor. Struck by two bombs and approximately six aerial torpedoes, the "Weevie" as she was nicknamed, was severely damaged, much more so than either the California or the Nevada. Two officers and 103 enlisted men lost their lives and the whole port side of the ship was virtually opened up. Massive patches constructed from underwater concrete enabled West Virginia to be refloated and drydocked. Extensive repairs at Pearl Harbor and later at Puget Sound Navy Yard enabled her to return to combat in July, 1944. West Virginia went on to earn five battle stars for WWII service.

Official Navy Photo

There were four U. S. Navy submarines in Pearl Harbor at the time of the attack: *Cachalot, Dolphin, Narwhal* and *Tautog.* All escaped damage as the attackers concentrated their strikes on the larger battleships and cruisers. *(USS Narwhal* (SS-167) is pictured in the foreground.) **Official Navy Photo**

The attack as seen from Aiea. Thick black smoke rises from the crippled battleships off Ford Island. **Official Navy Photo**

When the floating drydock sank, *Shaw,* with her bow section blown away by her exploding magazines, sank along with the drydock. However, her aft section was still buoyant and remained afloat. **Official Navy Photo**

Hundreds of five inch powder cases lay spent as sailors try to clear the decks of a destroyer during the height of the attack. **Official Navy Photo**

The battleship *Oklahoma* (left) has capsized. A tug and several smaller boats are at her side offering assistance and rescuing survivors. Sailors aboard the *Maryland* (center) pump water over the side in an attempt to keep her afloat. In the background, "Battleship Row" burns. **Official Navy Photo**

Seaplanes at Ford Island sit in ruins. **Official Navy Photo**

Berthed alongside the *Helena,* the minelayer *USS Oglala* (CM-4) was another of the ships sunk on December 7th. A torpedo, aimed at the cruiser *Helena,* ran underneath the *Oglala* and hit the *Helena.* But *Oglala* got the worst of it, for the force of the explosion against the *Helena* ruptured the old sides of the *Oglala.* Then a bomb dropped between the two ships did further damage, causing *Oglala* to lose all power. With the aid of passing tugs, she was moved to the dock astern of the *Helena* where she continued to flood. About two hours later, she capsized. (The *Helena* is pictured to the left of the capsized *Oglala.)* **Official Navy Photo**

While "Battleship Row" still burns, men on Ford Island begin cleaning up the debris and start the arduous job of salvaging their aircraft. **Official Navy Photo**

A PBY Catalina burning on the runway at the Kaneohe Naval Air Station. **Navy Photo/Kaneohe MCAS**

Privately owned vehicles did not escape the wrath of the attackers. **Navy Photo/Kaneohe MCAS**

The #3 gun crew of the *USS Ward* (DD-139) which fired the first shots of the war on December 7th. They spotted and shot at a submarine outside of Pearl Harbor hitting the conning tower. A depth charge attack finished off the intruder. **Official Navy Photo**

PACIFIC FLEET SHIPS PRESENT IN PEARL HARBOR ON
December 7, 1941

ALLEN (DD-66)	MEDUSA (AR-1)	SHAW (DD-373)
ANTARES (AKS-3)	MONAGHAN (DD-354)	SICARD (DM-21)
ARGONNE (AG-31)	MONTGOMERY (DM-17)	SOLACE (AH-5)
ARIZONA (BB-39)	MUGFORD (DD-389)	SOTOYOMO (YT-9)
ASH (YN-2)	NARWHAL (SS-167)	SUMNER (AG-32)
AVOCET (AVP-4)	NAVAJO (AT-64)	SUNNADIN (AT-28)
AYLWIN (DD-355)	NEOSHO (AO-23)	SWAN (AVP-7)
BAGLEY (DD-386)	NEVADA (BB-36)	TANEY (PG-37) (USCG)
BLUE (DD-387)	NEW ORLEANS (CA-32)	TANGIER (AV-8)
BOBOLINK (AM-20)	NOKOMIS (YT-142)	TAUTOG (SS-199)
BREESE (DM-18)	OGLALA (CM-4)	TENNESSEE (BB-43)
CG-8 (USCG)	OKLAHOMA (BB-37)	TERN (AM-31)
CACHALOT (SS-170)	ONTARIO (AT-13)	THORNTON (AVD-11)
CALIFORNIA (BB-44)	OSCEOLA (YT-129)	TIGER (PC-152) (USCG)
CASE (DD-370)	PT-20	TREVER (DMS-16)
CASSIN (DD-372)	PT-21	TRACY (DM-19)
CASTOR (AKS-1)	PT-22	TUCKER (DD-374)
CHENGHO (IX-52)	PT-23	TURKEY (AM-13)
CHEW (DD-106)	PT-24	UTAH (AG-16)
CINCHONA (YN-7)	PT-25	VEGA (AK-17)
COCKATOO (AMc-8)	PT-26	VESTAL (AR-4)
COCKENOE (YN-47)	PT-27	VIREO (AM-52)
CONDOR (AMc-14)	PT-28	WAPELLO (YN-56)
CONYNGHAM (DD-371)	PT-29	WARD (DD-139)
CROSSBILL (AMc-9)	PT-30	WASMUTH (DMS-15)
CUMMINGS (DD-365)	PT-42	WEST VIRGINIA (BB-48)
CURTISS (AV-4)	PATTERSON (DD-392)	WHITNEY (AD-4)
DALE (DD-353)	PELIAS (AS-14)	WIDGEON (ASR-1)
DETROIT (CL-8)	PENNSYLVANIA (BB-38)	WORDEN (DD-352)
DEWEY (DD-349)	PERRY (DMS-17)	YG-15
DOBBIN (AD-3)	PHELPS (DD-360)	YG-17
DOLPHIN (SS-169)	PHOENIX (CL-46)	YG-21
DOWNES (DD-375)	PREBLE (DM-20)	YMT-5
FARRAGUT (DD-348)	PRUITT (DM-22)	YNg-17
GAMBLE (DM-15)	PYRO (AE-1)	YO-21
GREBE (AM-43)	RAIL (AM-26)	YO-43
HELENA (CL-50)	RALEIGH (CL-7)	YP-108
HELM (DD-388)	RALPH TALBOT (DD-390)	YP-109
HENLEY (DD-391)	RAMAPO (AO-12)	YTT-3
HOGA (YT-146)	RAMSAY (DM-16)	YT-119
HONOLULU (CL-48)	REEDBIRD (AMc-30)	YT-130
HULBERT (AVD-6)	REID (DD-369)	YT-152
HULL (DD-350)	RELIANCE (USCG)	YT-153
JARVIS (DD-393)	RIGEL (AR-11)	YW-16
KEOSANGUA (AT-38)	ST. LOUIS (CL-49)	ZANE (DMS-14)
MAC DONOUGH (DD-351)	SACRAMENTO (PG-19)	YO-30
MANUWAI (YFB-17)	SAN FRANCISCO (CA-38)	YO-44
MARIN (YN-53)	SCHLEY (DD-103)	
MARYLAND (BB-46)	SELFRIDGE (DD-357)	

ARMY 228 Killed 364 Wounded		**NAVY** 2,004 Killed 710 Wounded
MARINES 109 Killed 69 Wounded		**CIVILIANS** 68 Killed 35 Wounded
	TOTALS 2,409 Killed 1,178 Wounded	

Compiled from official sources

SHIPS' POSITIONS ON DECEMBER 7th

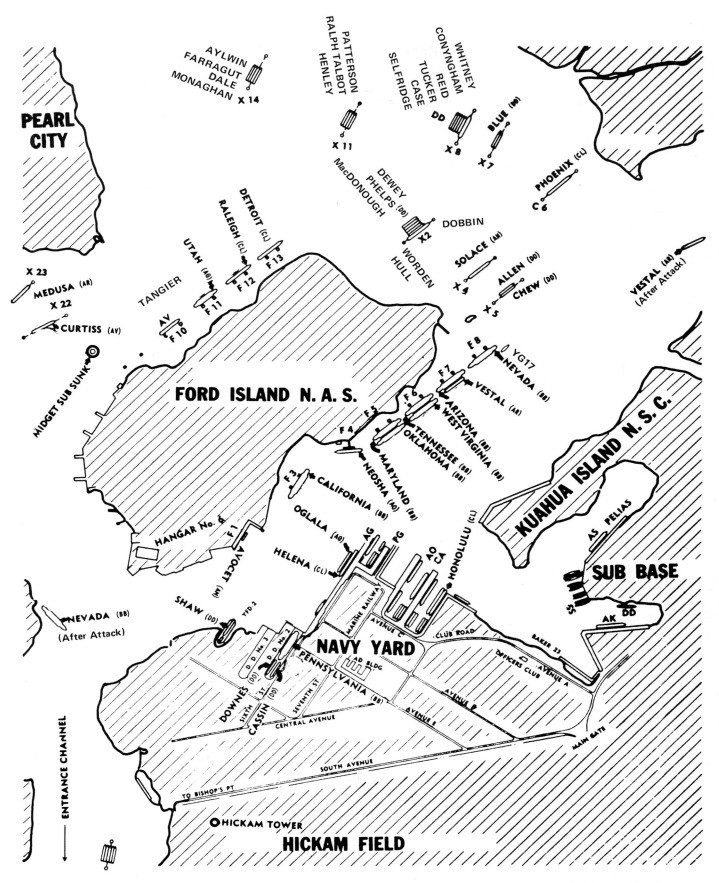

Compiled from official sources

AFTERMATH OF THE ATTACK

One of the 29 Japanese planes shot down.　**Official Navy Photo**

Burned-out tents at Wheeler Field following the attack.
Army Signal Corps

A General's staff car after being strafed by Japanese planes at Wheeler Field.　**Army Signal Corps**

Curtiss P-40 Warhawk pursuit planes and hangar at Wheeler Field after the attack.　**Army Signal Corps/Hickam AFB**

Of the 36 PBYs at Kaneohe, 27 were destroyed and 6 were damaged; the three saved were out on patrol.
Navy Photo/Kaneohe MCAS

Wrecked planes and equipment at the Kaneohe Naval Air Station.
Navy Photo/Kaneohe MCAS

Damaged military housing on the Pearl Harbor Naval Station following the attack.
Official Navy Photo

Civilian damage at McCully and King streets. When compared to military damage, civilian damage was slight. Most of the damage caused above occurred as a result of fire damage. Although three fires damaged an entire block in this district, the fire department concluded that one projectile started the first fire and that sparks probably caused the other two.

Werner Stoy/Camera Hawaii

USS Oklahoma, being outboard of the Maryland, never had a chance to fight. Within minutes after bombs began exploding on Ford Island, three torpedoes blasted huge holes in the Oklahoma and she immediately began listing heavily. Abandon ship was ordered and men began crawling over her starboard side as she was rolling. Two more torpedo hits caused Oklahoma to completely roll over within fifteen minutes of the start of the attack. Oklahoma lost 415 officers and men.

Official Navy Photo

The battleship USS Nevada, her decks a mass of wreckage, rests on the bottom of the shallow waters in Pearl Harbor.

Official Navy Photo

Japanese two-man submarine grounded on the beach at Bellows Field. One officer survived and became the first prisoner of WW-II.

Army Signal Corps/Hickam AFB

UNITED STATES NAVY

UNITED STATES MARINE CORPS

TO THE MEMORY OF THE GALLANT MEN
HERE ENTOMBED AND THEIR SHIPMATES
WHO GAVE THEIR LIVES IN ACTION
ON DECEMBER 7 1941 ON THE U.S.S. ARIZONA

Mass burial at the Kaneohe Naval Air Station for fallen comrades. **Navy Photo/Kaneohe MCAS**

A Japanese lieutenant who crashed near Kaneohe Bay is buried with honors despite the treachery of the attack.
Official Navy Photo

Sailors placing wreaths over graves of fellow shipmates killed during the Pearl Harbor attack. **Navy Photo/Kaneohe MCAS**

Downes (upright) and Cassin with the battleship Pennsylvania behind the two destroyers. The destroyers received the worst damage as they were subjected to nearly all types of damage — bomb hits, severe fires, explosions and fragmentation damage.

The hulls of both ships were scrapped in Pearl Harbor and their parts, machinery and useable fittings, were labelled and sent to Mare Island. There, the ships were literally put back together and later returned to fight the Japanese. **Official Navy Photo**

The USS Arizona as she appeared on December 10, 1941. **Official Navy Photo**

USS Cassin remains in a toppled state until her holes could be patched. Pennsylvania was taken out of drydock on December 12th. **National Archives**

SALVAGE OPERATIONS

Japanese midget submarine being salvaged from Pearl Harbor. Only one midget actually penetrated the harbor and it was sunk by a destroyer. **Official Navy Photo**

Rear view of a salvaged Japanese two-man submarine. *Curtiss,* a seaplane tender, scored two direct hits on the sub's conning tower. Later, the destroyer *Monaghan* depth charged the sub. Note the indentations on the sub caused by the depth charges. **Official Navy Photo**

Navy salvage crew lifts one of the twenty-nine Japanese aircraft shot down during the attack from waters of Pearl Harbor. **Official Navy Photo**

Originally thought to be a total loss, *Shaw* was "saved" by completely cutting off her bow and fabricating a new false bow. The Navy Yard then installed a temporary mast and control station and by February 9, 1942, *Shaw* departed under her own power for Mare Island Navy Yard in Northern California. By August of the same year, she was back at Pearl Harbor ready to enter the war in the Pacific. *Shaw* served the duration of World War II, earning a total of eleven battle stars. **Official Navy Photo**

False bow being fitted on the *USS Shaw* by Navy Yard workers. *Shaw* is in the drydock at left. **Official Navy Photo**

Lack of oxygen and the presence of hydrogen sulphide in many isolated compartments required divers to wear gas masks or other breathing apparatus. On February 7, 1942, two men were killed on the *Nevada* due to escaping gas from a confined compartment. The gas was hydrogen sulphide, and it is odorless in high concentrations. The interaction of stagnant water and paper products in pressurized spaces causes the gas to form. The divers pictured above took proper precautions.

Official Navy Photo

Divers emerging from the sunken *Arizona.* Nearly all of the survey work had to be performed by divers from inside the ship. Oil, ammunition and weaponry were gradually removed. Efforts to recover the dead had been abandoned as being too hazardous. It was decided that nothing further should be done to salvage *Arizona.* The ship would remain as a permanent memorial, not only to the 1177 crewman of the *Arizona,* but to all men who lost their lives on that "Day of Infamy." **Official Navy Photo**

The battleship *USS Nevada* entering dry dock on Feb. 18, 1942 after being refloated. She was the only battleship to get underway. When the attack came, *Nevada* was preparing to switch boilers, so she had two of her four boilers on line, the minimum required for a battleship to get underway. All the other battleships had only one boiler on line (the normal in-port procedure).

Official Navy Photo

Salvage work on the *USS California.* Because she had a list to port, counterflooding was resorted to in order to prevent the ship from capsizing as the *Oklahoma* had done. Divers plugged holes from the inside. Work progressed slowly in order to recover a number of bodies which still remained below decks.
Official Navy Photo

In order to salvage *California,* the ship had to be unloaded. This picture shows one of the ship's 14-inch guns being removed. All guns above the water level were removed as were other heavy objects such as safes, boats, cranes, anchors and anchor chain. Heavy machinery, oil, ammunition and supplies were also removed until on March 25, 1942, *California* was refloated and drydocked for repairs.
Official Navy Photo

On June 7, 1942, *California* prepares to leave drydock under her own power for Puget Sound Navy Yard. There a major reconstruction job was accomplished including improvements to her protection, stability, anti-aircraft battery and fire control system. In January of 1944, *California* departed Bremerton, Washington for shakedown cruises at San Pedro. In May, she sailed to participate in the invasion of the Marianas. Her heavy guns later paved the way for a number of assault landings, and *California* went on to earn seven battle stars for WWII service.
Official Navy Photo

Initially considered to be a total loss, it was proposed to dynamite the wrecked *Oglala* and use the pieces for urgently needed scrap. However, this plan had serious drawbacks due to the excess amount of time required for crane service and underwater divers experienced in cutting — their services were at a premium. Finally, it was decided to salvage the *Oglala.* Salvage pontoons (pictured above) were sunk and filled with compressed air; first to right the ship, then to refloat her, and finally to drydock her — a procedure that took about three months. **Official Navy Photo**

The raised *Oglala* prepared to sail under her own power following temporary repairs at the Pearl Harbor Navy Yard. The Los Angeles Shipbuilding Company refitted her as a repair vessel (ARG-1) and she was recommissioned February 28, 1944. *Oglala* returned to the central Pacific where she continued operations until the end of the war. **Official Navy Photo**

The righting of the *Oklahoma* was a precisely co-ordinated, slow process. Twenty-one electric shore winches anchored in concrete foundations on Ford Island were utilized. Because the winches had to be operated in unison, strain gauges were applied on the hauling wires at each strut and were carefully monitored. Models were constructed and tested before the actual righting began. The work started on March 8, 1943. **Official Navy Photo**

March 21, 1943 — *Oklahoma* slowly begins to rise. A highly effective air bubble, divided into five parts to prevent air pressure loss, considerably lightened the weight of the ship. Behaving in accordance with previous tests, *Oklahoma* was finally righted with a 2 degree list to port on June 16, 1943.

Official Navy Photo

Oklahoma in drydock after being stripped of her guns and auxiliary machinery. Because of the extensive damage originally caused, there was no thought to return the ship to active service. *Oklahoma* was decommissioned on September 1, 1944 and sold for scrap in December of 1946. On May 10, 1947, she left Pearl Harbor in tow for the west coast. However, on May 17, during a storm at sea, the tow line parted and *Oklahoma* plunged to the depths of the Pacific. **Official Navy Photo**

The battleship *USS Washington* in drydock on February 23, 1944. *Washington* was not involved in the Pearl Harbor attack. Rather, this damage occurred off Kwajalein Atoll when *Washington* rammed *Indiana* as she cut across *Washington's* bow. Operating in total darkness, *Indiana* was dropping out of formation to fuel escorting destroyers. This photo illustrates the monumental jobs assigned the Pearl Harbor Naval Shipyard. *Washington* was fitted with a temporary bow and later received permanent repairs at Puget Sound. **Official Navy Photo**

CHA III- PEARL HARBOR BANNER ★ DECEMBER 7, 1945   Page 7

7000

Yard Repair Record Is Magnificent

Seven thousand ships . . . large and small fighting ships . . . a mighty armada that brought victory in the Pacific . . . this was the amazing record of ships repaired at the Pearl Harbor Navy Yard during the war, and returned to action by the sweat and labor of Navy Yard employees.

Fleet Admiral Chester W. Nimitz, USN, Commander-in-Chief, Pacific Ocean Area, paid tribute to the Yard workers a few months before the Japs surrendered, when he declared that "at no time did the Navy Yard employees fail to restore a damaged ship to the fighting line on schedule."

Because of Pearl Harbor's strategic and advanced location, ships were returned to the Fleet in ten days; in two weeks shorter time than if repaired in West Coast yards.

A number of ships have been to the Yard two and three times for damage repairs and have gone forth again to the far Western Pacific to continue the fight against Japan.

Miraculous repair jobs were performed by the workers as they rushed to meet time schedules. Remembered most in the minds of the workmen was the carrier Yorktown.

When the flattop pulled into Pearl Harbor in the summer of 1942, she was badly damaged, from a direct bomb-hit which had pierced and finally exploded in the bowels of the ship, six decks down; from a second bomb which caromed off her flight gallery forward on the starboard side and exploded upon hitting the water, peppering the hull above the water-line with shrapnel and from a third near miss which exploded in the water close enough to the side to open the seams and corrugate the bottom on the port side amidships.

Inside the vessel, more than 1400 men—shipfitters, machinists, welders, electricians, and shipwrights worked on the different levels to restore the ship's structural strength and as this work proceeded to renew or replace the instruments, electric wiring, and fixtures which had been damaged in the blast.

Four days after she had arrived at the Navy Yard, the Yorktown was again a fighting ship and had joined Admiral Nimitz's force which was within 200 miles of the enemy off Midway.

To accomplish such remarkable feats, the Navy Yard expanded four and five times its original number of shops and employees. From a mere 5,000 workers before the war, the Yard recruited more men and women, largely from the mainland, to increase its personnel to over 28,000.

New piers and wharves have been built and a number of graving docks and a marine railway have been added to the Yard's facilities. Several hundred ships are accommodated by the piers and anchorages at Pearl Harbor. Several times entrances and exits in one day totaled over 280.

With this expansion of men and Yard facilities the Navy Yard was able to turn out almost any task which confronted them. A cruiser was completely repaired structurally and made ready for sea in 14 days, after having been hit in the fore and stern, two aircraft carriers with more than ten regular days work on each were made ready for action in 72 hours; and the battlewagon, USS Maryland, which the Japs twice claimed sunk, once on December 7, 1941 and again in 1945, damaged while supporting landing operations in the Philippines, was completely rebuilt from the forecastle to the third deck, 30 days below the end of the time allowed for its repair.

Barrage Balloon at Pearl Harbor

THIS IS THE FIRST photograph ever published by the Banner showing the big barrage balloons which were placed at strategic points throughout the Pearl Harbor area to discourage any attempts at low bombing which the Japanese might have tried during the war. This balloon was located in the Hickam end of Civilian Housing Area III. The big bags were placed around the harbor in 1942, and removed some months later. There was no attack while they were placed. Occasionally, all balloons were raised simultaneously during tests, and the Pearl Harbor sky was an unusual sight at such times.

Remember The USS Pensacola?

ONE OF the biggest jobs ever attempted at Pearl Harbor was the repair of the cruiser USS Pensacola. The work took nine months to complete and the job was made more difficult by the Japs but managed to reach Pearl Harbor, although the deck was only four feet above water. The torpedo killed hundreds, and many men were trapped and died when the after compartments were closed off to save the vessel. Here we see part of the ship as it appeared shortly after work was started on the repair of the vessel. The torpedo hit below this point. Notice the bulge on the right.

Article in the Pearl Harbor Banner describing the amazing record of the Pearl Harbor Naval Yard in repairing 7,000 ships during the war. **Official Navy Photo**

The sunken remains of the *USS Utah*. Because she was used as a target ship for aircraft and since she did not occupy an essential berth in her capsized position, a low priority was assigned to the salvage of the *Utah*. The ship was partly righted and her ordnance material was removed. However, future salvage work was deemed uneconomical and no further work was performed on her. Since some fifty-eight men were still entombed in the *Utah,* it was later decided that *Utah* remain where she was. A memorial was constructed on Ford Island and formally dedicated May 27, 1972. Utah Senator Frank E. Moss was the guest speaker. **Official Navy Photo**

Honolulu Star-Bulletin 1st EXTRA

Evening Bulletin, Est. 1882, No. 11287
Hawaiian Star, Vol. XLVIII No. 15309

HONOLULU, TERRITORY OF HAWAII, U. S. A., SUNDAY, DECEMBER 7, 1941 ★ PRICE FIVE CENTS

WAR !

(Associated Press by Transpacific Telephone)

SAN FRANCISCO, Dec. 7.—President Roosevelt announced this morning that Japanese planes had attacked Manila and Pearl Harbor.

OAHU BOMBED BY JAPANESE PLANES

SIX KNOWN DEAD, 21 INJURED, AT EMERGENCY HOSPITAL

Honolulu Star-Bulletin/Branch 46, FRA

A grim President Roosevelt, wearing a black armband as a symbol of national mourning for those killed at Pearl Harbor the day before, signs the formal declaration of war against Japan. On December 8, 1941, President Franklin Delano Roosevelt addressed a joint session of the House and Senate asking for a declaration of war against Japan. He spoke for only six minutes, and when he had finished, he received an ovation like none he had received in his eight years as President. Being no debate, the formal declaration of war was delivered to and signed by the President two and one-half hours after his message to Congress. **Department of the Interior**

On the morning of December 31, 1941, Admiral Nimitz assumed command of the Pacific Fleet in ceremonies aboard the submarine *Grayling* moored at the Submarine Base in Pearl Harbor. Nimitz took command at a time when morale at Pearl Harbor was rapidly deteriorating. Nimitz's primary tasks were to guard the Hawaiian Islands including Midway, to protect shipping between Hawaii and the mainland and between the United States and Australia, and to guard Samoa. **Official Navy Photo**

Army tanks guard the entrance to Iolani Palace which housed many important government offices. Expecting an invasion and possible future attacks, Martial Law was declared in the after-noon of December 7th. It lasted for nearly three years.
Werner Stoy/Camera Hawaii

Memorial services for Pearl Harbor casualties held January 1, 1942 at Oahu Cemetery in Nuuanu Valley. Army dead were buried in the cemetery at Schofield Barracks while Navy dead were buried at Oahu Cemetery, Kaneohe Bay and at Red Hill near Aiea.
Werner Stoy/Camera Hawaii

Barbed wire was strung on nearly all beaches, including Waikiki Beach, in anticipation of an invasion which the Japanese never planned. Sun-bathers in this picture use the barbed wire to dry their wet bathing accessories. The Royal Hawaiian Hotel stands out in the background in this early 1942 photo.
Werner Stoy/Camera Hawaii

Early in the war, everyone in the territory was issued an Army gas mask along with instructions on how to wear it. Countless bomb shelters were built and strict black-out procedures were enforced.   **Werner Stoy/Camera Hawaii**

Citizens attempting to book passage out of Honolulu shortly after war was declared. During the first few months of the war, close to 30,000 people were evacuated to the mainland, most of them being military dependents and Island women and children. Long waiting lists developed and priorities were established. However, after the Battle of Midway in June, 1942, many citizens cancelled their reservations. Feeling secure again, few new applications were received despite renewed appeals by the military governor.   **Werner Stoy/Camera Hawaii**

On May 27, 1942, Admiral Nimitz presented awards to heroes of the early phases of the war. The ceremonies took place aboard the carrier *USS Enterprise.* Note the *Oklahoma* still

capsized and salvage operations being conducted on the *West Virginia* in the background.   **Official Navy Photo**

Hawaii's money supply quickly changed. In order to prevent hoarding and to keep large amounts out of the hands of foreign agents and possible invaders, a new issue of currency appeared. Imprinted with "HAWAII" on the obverse and reverse and having the serial numbers and seal in a different color (brown),

the new currency was used between July, 1942 and October, 1944. The regular currency that was exchanged for the new bills was burned under the supervision of a committee representing the major Honolulu banks. (Shown smaller than actual size)   **Pearlridge Stamp and Coin**

USO show at Kahuku, July 2, 1942. Note the sign behind the hula dancer. As the number of military men stationed in and around Honolulu or just passing through swelled into the hundreds of thousands by 1944 and 1945, social values changed and interracial marriages zoomed despite military braking efforts. Friction between local and mainland young men increased as many Island girls changed allegiance to the glamour and easy money of the mainland strangers.

Army Signal Corps/Univ. of Hawaii Archives

On the first anniversary of the Pearl Harbor attack, the Japanese government issued a commemorative stamp in honor of their victories in the "Greater East Asia War." Another stamp in the set honored the victories in the Burma Campaign. (Stamp shown larger than actual size.)

Pacific Medals

Historic picture of Pearl Harbor taken December 12, 1943 after the Fleet returned from the invasion of the Gilbert Islands on November 20th. Over 150 ships are in the harbor, including seven carriers, six battleships, twelve cruisers, thirty-one destroyers, twenty-two submarines, plus transports, cargo ships and LST's preparing for the Kwajalein Atoll operation.

Official Navy Photo

War bond sales booth. Boom conditions and a short supply of luxury goods spurred bond sales. Sales on special occasions such as the anniversary of Pearl Harbor caused sales to zoom four and five times the goals set. Based on dollars per person, the 14th Naval District was always near the top in competition with other naval establishments throughout the country and often won first place. **Honolulu Advertiser/Univ. of Hawaii Archives**

Hundreds of thousands of troops passed through Pearl Harbor to receive advance training, provisions and equipment or simply to wait for transit to the forward areas of the war.

Official Navy Photo

Ships, landing craft, tanks, trucks and other components of modern warfare continually passed through Pearl Harbor on their way to the battle front. **Official Navy Photo**

General Douglas MacArthur, President Franklin D. Roosevelt and Admiral Chester W. Nimitz aboard the cruiser *USS Baltimore* at Pearl Harbor, July 26, 1944. Roosevelt came to Hawaii to attend a conference to map the Formosa and China offensive. However, because this plan called for almost 700,000 men, the proposed offensive was later cancelled. Instead, Iwo Jima and Okinawa were selected for the offensive, and MacArthur was ordered to proceed with the return to the Philippines.

Official Navy Photo

Panorama view of Halawa Naval Cemetery in the hillside above Pearl Harbor. Memorial services are being held on Memorial Day, 1945. The graves decorated with flowers contain those who died on December 7, 1941.   **Official Navy Photo**

On August 14, 1945, after several unofficial reports had been made, the official report that the Japanese had surrendered was announced. Air-raid sirens wailed, church bells pealed and alarms clanged. Sailors, marines, soldiers and civilians "invaded" the streets of downtown Honolulu celebrating the restoration of peace. Traffic slowed to a standstill.

Earl J. Stephenson/Univ. of Hawaii Archives

Officers and enlisted men display a new found spirit of camaraderie as the hardships of the past are temporarily forgotten in the joy and excitement of the present.

Earl J. Stephenson/Univ. of Hawaii Archives

Jubilant sailors wave to the photographer as an impromptu "ticker-tape" parade is in progress.

Werner Stoy/Camera Hawaii

Units of the U. S. Pacific Fleet assemble in Sagami Bay (Japan) on the morning of September 2, 1945 for the formal Japanese surrender. Mt. Fuji is in the background. **Official Navy Photo**

With General MacArthur and Admirals Halsey and Forrest Sherman standing directly behind him, Fleet Admiral Chester W. Nimitz signs the Japanese surrender document on board the *USS Missouri* in Tokyo Bay on September 2, 1945.

Official Navy Photo

USS Tinosa (SS-283) steams into Pearl Harbor with battle flags flying following the formal end of the war in 1945.
Official Navy Photo

Searchlight display staged by 130 ships of the U. S. Pacific Fleet in Pearl Harbor on a clear moonlit night in the late 1940's.
Official Navy Photo

Members of the 442nd combat team, veterans of the European and Italian campaigns, prepare to disembark from their transport after an arduous journey from New York (August 9, 1946). The acclaim achieved by the AJA's (Americans of Japanese Ancestry) plus a lack of proven sabotage rebuilt public confidence in the Japanese community which comprised a significant portion of Hawaii's population.
Army Signal Corps/Univ. of Hawaii Archives

USS ARIZONA MEMORIAL

The final resting place for 1,102 American servicemen. *Arizona's* anti-aircraft batteries, ammunition, salvageable machinery and topsides were gradually removed and all projections from the hull were cut off by divers. In 1950, a temporary memorial platform was built above the ship's main deck house. Work toward a permanent memorial got underway in 1958 when the Navy asked the Pacific War Memorial Commission to take on the task of raising money to build a new memorial.

Official Navy Photo

USS Bennington (CVS-20) renders honors to the once proud battleship *USS Arizona.* During Memorial Day weekend in 1958, 1102 Naval and Marine Corps officers and enlisted men assembled on the flight deck of the *Bennington* to form "ARIZONA" in tribute to the 1102 shipmates entombed in the sunken battleship.

Official Navy Photo

Workmen hoist one of the two 250-ton concrete girders that will support the memorial. The girders rest on 36 pre-stressed pilings that were driven into the harbor bottom.

Official Navy Photo

Early stage of construction on the memorial (Nov. 28, 1960). Construction of the memorial was authorized by the 85th Congress and approved by President Eisenhower in 1958. A bill appropriating $150,000 was passed by the 87th Congress and signed by President Kennedy in 1961. Under sponsorship of the Pacific War Memorial Commission, the remaining funds were raised. $100,000 came from the State of Hawaii, and the balance of $250,000 came from public contributions with assists from a Ralph Edwards ("This is Your Life") television program and an Elvis Presley show, both of which were produced in Hawaii.

Official Navy Photo

The memorial nears completion. Being an enclosed bridge, the memorial spans the sunken hull of the battleship *USS Arizona*. No part of the memorial touches the sunken ship. The memorial is 184 feet long, and varies in width from 27 feet at the center to 36 feet at the ends. Its height varies from 14 feet at the center to 21 feet at the ends. The memorial was dedicated on Memorial Day, 1962. **Official Navy Photo**

"The form, wherein the structure sags in the center but stands strong and vigorous at the ends, expresses initial defeat and ultimate victory.

"Wide openings in walls and roof permit a flooding by sunlight and a close view of the sunken battleship eight feet below, both fore and aft. At low tide, as the sun shines upon the hull, the barnacles which encrust it shimmer like gold jewels . . . a beautiful sarcophagus.

"The overall effect is one of serenity. Overtones of sadness have been omitted to permit the individual to contemplate his own personal responses . . . his innermost feelings."

Alfres Preis, Architect.   **Official Navy Photo**

The flagpole on which the American flag flies is mounted on a portion of the ship's super-structure and does not touch any part of the memorial itself. The memorial is divided into three sections: a museum room, the assembly area (shown above) which can accommodate 200 people for ceremonies, and the shrine room. **Official Navy Photo**

Ship's bell with the following inscription: "This ship's bell from the *USS Arizona* was brought up from the floor of Pearl Harbor by U. S. Navy divers. The battleship was torpedoed on December 7, 1941." The bell was originally presented to the state of Arizona where it was on display at the University of Arizona. In 1966, Arizona's then Governor Paul Fannin returned the bell to the Navy, and it was installed in the museum room of the Arizona Memorial on a base of Vermont marble. Chief Warrant Officer, John H. McCarron, one of the few survivors of *Arizona's* 1550 man crew, unveiled the bell at ceremonies conducted aboard the memorial on Memorial Day, 1966.

Dick Wisniewski/Pacific Medals

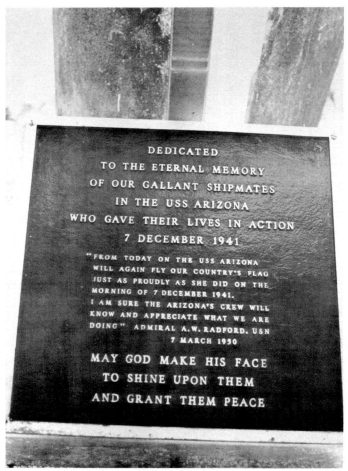

Dedication plaque authorizing the American flag to be flown over the sunken remains of the *USS Arizona.* Although the *Arizona* is no longer in commission (she was stricken from the active list in 1942), the Navy granted special permission to fly the American flag over the *Arizona* in memory of the brave men who lost their lives on that tragic Sunday morning.

Dick Wisniewski/Pacific Medals

Plaque on board the memorial listing all the Commanding Officers of *Arizona* from the time she was commissioned until she was sunk. The great seal of the state of Arizona is above the engraved listing.

Dick Wisniewski/Pacific Medals

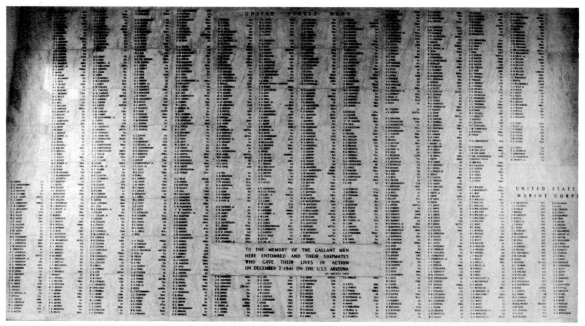

Shrine room aboard the USS Arizona Memorial listing the 1177 names of *Arizona's* crewmen killed in the December 7, 1941 attack. Only 75 bodies were ever recovered, and the remaining 1102 are still entombed in the sunken battleship.

Official Navy Photo

Hand-carved insignia of the Pearl Harbor Survivors Association now hanging in the museum room of the Arizona Memorial. The insignia was installed in the memorial prior to Memorial Day ceremonies in 1977. **Photo by Author**

USS Arizona Memorial plaque presented to Admiral Persons by Mr. Tarlou, President of the Jewish War Veterans.
Official Navy Photo

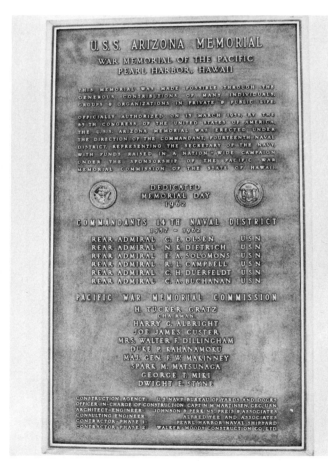

Dedication plaque for the USS Arizona Memorial. Dedication services took place at 9:30 a.m., Wednesday, May 30 (Memorial Day), 1962 formally paying tribute to the once proud battleship, the men entombed within, and to all others who died on that "Day of Infamy" December 7, 1941. **Photo by Author**

Police Officer Fred Kukonu (Narrator/Historian aboard the Arizona Memorial) tells visitors to the memorial how he witnessed the collapse of *Arizona's* ventilator shaft the day before (Wednesday, June 1, 1977). The interaction of seawater on the hull of the sunken battleship is gradually eating away the metal.
Official Navy Photo

SCALE MODEL OF THE USS ARIZONA (BB-39)

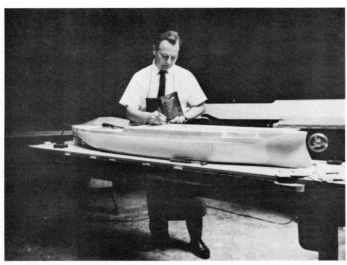

An employee of Boucher-Lewis of New York, a precision model builder, is shown working on the initial phase of the *Arizona* scale model. Pearl Harbor Branch 46, Fleet Reserve Association, conceived the idea of building the scale model and conducted a fund drive among the association's membership.

Boucher-Lewis/Branch 46, FRA

Constructed of kiln-dried wood and non-ferrous metals, the completed model measured six feet, three inches in length and weighed 325 pounds. It was built to exact specifications using official Navy blueprints.   **Boucher-Lewis/Branch 46, FRA**

The scale model of the *USS Arizona* (photographed outside of its protective case) cost $7,500 and is precise down to the smallest porthole.   **Official Navy Photo**

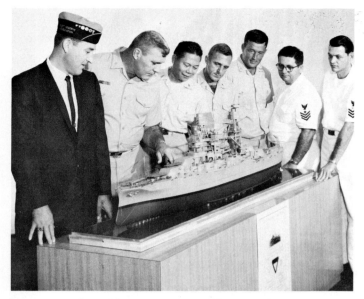

Members of Pearl Harbor Branch 46, Fleet Reserve Association, inspect the scale model of the *USS Arizona* after its long journey from the east coast. Left to right are: Phil Shear (DM1), then President, C. E. Burns (BMC), Joseph Depositor (DKC), "Skip" Ogilbie (SKC), Ebb Hall (YNC), Frank Ott (DM1) and Lloyd Ashley (PR1). **Official Navy Photo**

Formal dedication ceremonies for the scale model of the *USS Arizona.* President Bernard P. O'Hare of the Fleet Reserve Association officially turned the scale model over to Rear Admiral Richard B. Lynch in ceremonies aboard the Arizona Memorial on December 7, 1967. **Official Navy Photo**

With its air-tight case, stainless steel base and formica covered display stand, the total project cost almost $10,000. **Official Navy Photo**

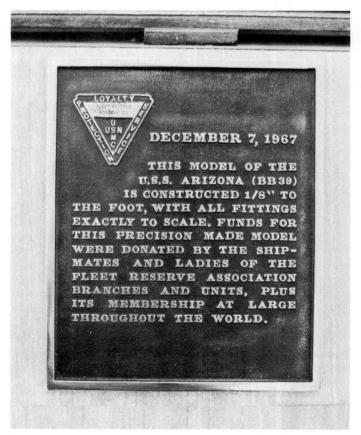

Dedication plaque for the scale model of the *USS Arizona.* **Dick Wisniewski/Pacific Medals**

ANCHOR MEMORIALS

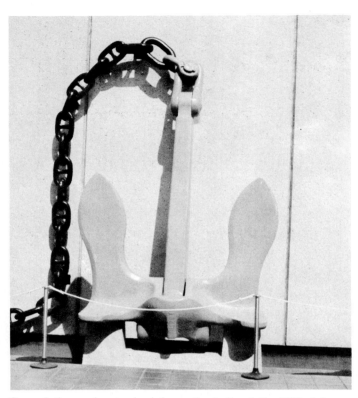

One of the anchors raised from the hulk of the USS Arizona. Cast in Chester, Pennsylvania in 1911, the anchor weighs 19,585 pounds. This anchor is prominently displayed at the entrance to the USS Arizona Memorial Visitor Center.　**Photo by Author**

Fred Kukonu (right), Narrator/Historian of the USS Arizona Memorial, presents a flag previously flown over the memorial to the late Arizona Governor Wes Bolin. In the background, is another of the *USS Arizona's* anchors which was made into a memorial to honor the ship's crewmen. Dedicated on December 7, 1976, the memorial is located on the grounds of the state capital at Phoenix.
　Phoenix Republic & Gazette Photo courtesy of Fred Kukonu

Anchor cross on the face of the altar at St. George's Episcopal Church at Pearl Harbor.　**Photo by Author**

THE ANCHOR CROSS ON THE ALTAR IS CONSTRUCTED OF STEEL FROM THE USS ARIZONA SUNK AT PEARL HARBOR 7 DEC 1941

HOPE IS AN ANCHOR OF THE SOUL BOTH SURE AND STEADFAST

HEBREWS 6 19

Plaque on the sanctuary wall at St. George's identifying the anchor cross. Although it shines like silver, it is actually made from steel that was removed from the USS Arizona during salvage operations.　**Photo by Author**

NATIONAL MEMORIAL CEMETERY OF THE PACIFIC

The Mausoleum at Pearl Harbor, January 5, 1949. The first group of caskets bearing the remains of World War II dead are being readied for shipment to the National Memorial Cemetery of the Pacific. **Army Signal Corps/Cemetery Collection**

Burial services at the National Memorial Cemetery on February 2, 1949. One casket is brought forward as a symbol of the entire group of 216. The flags, which previously covered the caskets, are packed in cellophane bags and placed at the head of each casket.

The remains of famed war correspondent Ernest T. Pyle were reinterred in the National Cemetery on July 19, 1949. **Army Signal Corps/Cemetery Collection**

Clergymen of the Catholic, Jewish and Protestant Faiths are shown administering last rites in this February 24th photo. The flag handlers and color guard were from the Submarine Base at Pearl Harbor. The remains of nearly 13,000 World War II servicemen comprised the initial burials in the cemetery. Formal dedication services were held on September 2, 1949, the fourth anniversary of V-J Day. **Army Signal Corps/Cemetery Collection**

The National Memorial Cemetery of the Pacific is located in Punchbowl Crater, a long-extinct volcano. Its Hawaiian name, "Puowaina," means "Consecrated Hill" or "Hill of Sacrifice." Many secret burials of Alii (royalty) were held in the crater. Also, offenders of Hawaiian taboos were sacrificed in the crater. Prior to the war, it was used by the Hawaii National Guard as a training ground. During the war, it served as an observation and fire control station for the harbor defense system. In 1943, the Governor of Hawaii, with the approval of the legislature, offered the Punchbowl area to the War Department for use as a national cemetery. Lacking sufficient funds, the actual establishment of the cemetery was delayed until after the conclusion of the war. On January 4, 1949, an unknown serviceman killed in the Pearl Harbor attack became the first interment in the cemetery. **U. S. Army Photo/Cemetery Collection**

The American Battle Monuments Commission erected a memorial at the cemetery. It was officially dedicated on May 1, 1966. It consists of a chapel, a gallery of mosaic mural maps of the Pacific theaters of action during World War II and the Korean conflict, and a monumental stairway bordered by eight marble walls called the "Courts of the Missing." On these walls are engraved the names of 26,280 American servicemen ". . . whose earthly resting place is known only to God."

Annual ceremonies include an Easter sunrise service and the Hawaiian Folk Mass. Special ceremonies are held on Veterans Day, Memorial Day and December 7th.

U. S. Army Photo/Cemetery Collection

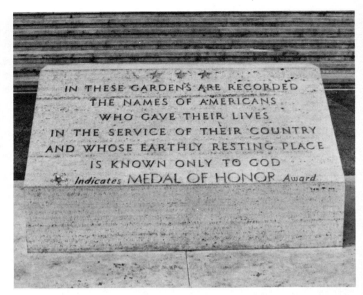

Marble plaque at the foot of the stairway leading to the "Courts of the Missing." **Dick Wisniewski/Pacific Medals**

Every five years, the Pearl Harbor Survivors Association holds its annual convention in Hawaii to pay special homage to their fallen shipmates. National officers of the association present a wreath at ceremonies held at the National Memorial Cemetery of the Pacific. At the same time, services are also held aboard the Arizona Memorial. The officers (left to right) are: Fred R. McEnany (Secretary), George E. Slavens (Vice-President), H. F. Garbuschewski (Convention Coordinator), Joel E. Bachner (President) and Jesse E. Pond, Jr. (Treasurer).

Henry C. T. Chang/Pearl Harbor Survivors Assoc.

The 30 foot sculptured figure of Columbia with laurel branch standing on the symbolized prow of a Navy carrier, is proclaiming President Abraham Lincoln's words to a bereaved mother: "THE SOLEMN PRIDE THAT MUST BE YOURS TO HAVE LAID SO COSTLY A SACRIFICE UPON THE ALTAR OF FREEDOM." **U. S. Army Photo/Cemetery Collection**

DECEMBER 7th MEMORIAL SERVICES

President Gerald Ford visited the Arizona Memorial on December 7, 1975, thereby becoming the first President to visit the memorial on an anniversary of the attack. **Official Navy Photo**

Memorial services aboard the Arizona Memorial. Two official ceremonies are held each year: Memorial Day and December 7th. On these special occasions, as many as 15 separate patriotic organizations attend the memorial services and present wreaths to honor their deceased members. These groups include the Fleet Reserve Association, the Veterans of Foreign Wars, Disabled American Veterans, American Legion, Pearl Harbor Survivors Association and Gold Star Mothers just to name a few. In addition, smaller groups frequently hold private ceremonies throughout the year. **Dick Wisniewski/Pacific Medals**

Members of the Pearl Harbor Survivors Association are among the approximately 200 people attending memorial services aboard the Arizona Memorial on December 7, 1976, the 35th anniversary of the Pearl Harbor attack.
Henry C. T. Chang/Pearl Harbor Survivors Association

UTAH MEMORIAL

The Utah Memorial on the opposite side of Ford Island. Utah Senator Frank E. Moss was the guest speaker at dedication ceremonies held May 27, 1972. **Official Navy Photo**

NEAR THIS SPOT, AT BERTH FOX 11, ON THE MORNING OF 7 DECEMBER 1941, THE USS UTAH WAS STRUCK ON THE PORTSIDE WITH WHAT IS BELIEVED TO HAVE BEEN THREE AERIAL TORPEDOES AND WAS SUNK. SHE WAS SUBSEQUENTLY ROLLED OVER TO CLEAR THE CHANNEL BUT WAS LEFT ON THE BOTTOM.

Utah Memorial dedication plaque on Ford Island.
Official Navy Photo

"THE LONELY ONE" - KAMEHAMEHA (SSB(N)-642)

Kamehameha (SSB(N)-642) in the Pearl Harbor channel. The fleet ballistic missile submarine is named after a Hawaiian king and warrior whose name means "the lonely one." Kamehameha conquered the islands and united them under one kingdom. By the time of his death in 1819, he had established a stable government, ended feudal wars and restored the islands' shattered economy. The Polaris Submarine Kamehameha was launched January 16, 1965 under the sponsorship of Mrs. Samuel Wilder King, widow of Captain King (governor of Hawaii from 1953 to 1957). Commissioned December 10, 1965, Kamehameha silently and invisibly roams the seas on her assigned patrols. **Official Navy Photo**

Arizona II

Mrs. Esther Ross Hoggan formally christens *Arizona II* with a sprinkling of champagne as Don Stevens, Past President of Branch 46, FRA, looks on. Dedication ceremonies took place on October 17, 1977, the 61st anniversary of the commissioning of the original *Arizona*. Mrs. Hoggan (then Miss Esther Ross, daughter of a pioneer Arizona family) christened the original *USS Arizona* on June 19, 1915 at the New York Navy Yard. This was Mrs. Hoggan's first visit to Pearl Harbor and the final resting place of the *USS Arizona*.   **Official Navy Photo**

The Starr family with a representative of the Arizona Memorial Museum Foundation which organized the dedication ceremonies: (left to right) Mr. Leon Starr, his mother Marie Starr, Gloria May (Foundation representative), wife Evelyn and son Ronald. Mr. Starr has been building models of one type or another in his spare time since childhood. The entire family shared in the production of *Arizona II* in one way or another from applying the many coats of paint to sewing canvas. *Arizona II* is now at Pearl Harbor, exactly where Leon Starr hoped it would finally be when he received his initial inspiration to build the model battleship.   **Photo by Author**

Arizona II, a 27 foot scale model of the original *Arizona,* was constructed entirely by hand by Mr. Leon Starr and his family. After a careful study of every available photograph of the *USS Arizona,* the Starr family set to work on the replica in August, 1976. Three months later, the finished model proved its seaworthiness by sailing at Marina Del Ray, California during December 7th ceremonies. *Arizona II* is accurate in every detail from fire axes and fire hoses, cable and switch boxes, to moveable guns and search lights and 360 portholes in her hull. The model is constructed of fiberglass, polyester and wood. Pending construction of a permanent shelter for *Arizona II,* the model will be kept in storage to protect it from the elements. It will be displayed at special occasions such as parades and memorial ceremonies.   **Official Navy Photo**

VISITOR CENTER

Rev. Dr. Abraham K. Akaka, Pastor of Honolulu's historic Kawaiahao Church, sprinkles holy water on the groundbreaking site for the new USS Arizona Memorial Visitor Center. He is using a green ti leaf in this traditional Hawaiian blessing. Rear Admiral R.A. Wentworth, Jr., USN, Commander of the Pearl Harbor Naval Base, presided at the groundbreaking ceremony held on October 19, 1978. Rear Admiral Wentworth is pictured holding the koa wood bowl of holy water. Other prominently pictured speakers in the front row are, left to right: U.S. Senator Spark M. Matsunaga; Hawaii Governor George R. Ariyoshi; and Admiral Donald C. Davis, USN, Commander in Chief, U.S. Pacific Fleet, who gave the keynote address. A scale model of the proposed facility is in the foreground.   **Photo by Author**

Mr. Ansil "Sandy" Saunders, President of the Arizona Memorial Museum Foundation, turns a spadeful of ground with the ceremonial shovel. Other groundbreakers pictured behind Mr. Saunders waiting their turns are, left to right: Mr. George Slavens of the Pearl Harbor Survivors Association; former State Senator David McClung (blocked by Mr. Saunders); State Representative Faith P. Evans; Rear Admiral N.W. Clements, CEC, USN, the Navy's top engineer in the Pacific; and U.S. Congressman Cecil Heftel. A total of fifteen groundbreakers participated in the ceremony. The remainder of the groundbreakers included: Senator Matsunaga; Governor Ariyoshi; Admiral Davis; Rear Admiral E. Alvey Wright, USN (Ret.), who represented U.S. Senator Daniel K. Inouye; U.S. Congressman Daniel K. Akaka; Rear Admiral Wentworth; Mr. Robert Barrel of the National Park Service; Mr. Donald D. Chapman, the center's architect; and Mr. Gerard Sakamoto, the contractor.   **Photo by Author**

Rear Admiral Clements autographs the handle of the groundbreaking shovel. Each of the other groundbreaking participants also autographed the ceremonial shovel for later display in the new visitor center. Two Navy Seabees forged the shovel from a piece of steel plating salvaged from the sunken hulk of the USS Arizona.   **Photo by Author**

Construction photo of the new visitor center. When the USS Arizona Memorial opened in 1962, Navy and civilian boats brought 209,361 visitors. By the end of the decade, the visitor count had exceeded 600,000. Visitor growth continued into the next decade, surpassing 1,000,000 in 1973 and every year thereafter.   **Photo by Author**

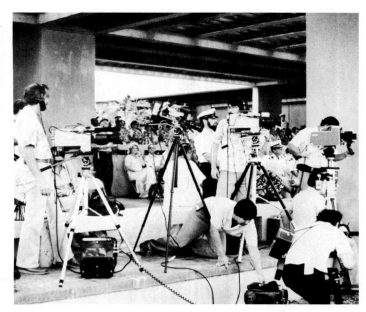

In ceremonies held on December 7, 1979, Ansil "Sandy" Saunders presents Rear Admiral Edward S. Briggs, Commander of the Pearl Harbor Naval Base, a cake representing a check for $456,484.25. The "check" was the final installment of nearly $1 million in donations raised by the Arizona Memorial Museum Foundation for the new visitor center. Individual donations raised by the Foundation exceeded $500,000. Other major donations were provided by the State of Hawaii, the Pearl Harbor Survivors Association, the national membership of the Fleet Reserve Association, the Disabled American Veterans, and the National Ladies Auxiliary of the Fleet Reserve Association.
Photo by Author

Camera crews from all of Honolulu's major television stations prepare to record the dedication ceremonies for the new USS Arizona Memorial Visitor Center on October 10, 1980. This date marked the culmination of the hopes and dreams of many groups and individuals who struggled for more than ten years to bring about this event. Since 1968, numerous bills had been introduced in Congress allocating funds for the proposed center, but none passed. Finally, in July of 1978, after years of planning, negotiations, and fund raising efforts, Hawaii's U.S. Senators obtained the project's full approval under the Military Construction Program.
Photo by Author

Lei and ribbon cutting ceremony for the new visitor center. Pictured above are, left to right: Admiral Issac C. Kidd, Jr., USN (Ret.), son of Rear Admiral Kidd who was killed aboard the USS Arizona during the Pearl Harbor attack; Governor Ariyoshi; and Rev. Akaka. In a custody transfer ceremony a few minutes earlier, the U.S. Navy relinquished jurisdiction over the memorial and visitor center, turning over the responsibility to the National Park Service. However, the Navy continued to provide shuttle boat service from the visitor center to the memorial and back.
Photo by Author

Ceremonial cake depicting the USS Arizona Memorial. The Pearl Harbor Submarine Base Enlisted Dining Facility provided the cake which was the centerpiece of a small, informal post-dedication party. As a result of the close cooperation between the U.S. Navy and the National Park Service, the new $5 million visitor center was designed to accommodate more than 3,000 visitors per day and at the same time to eliminate the long, sometimes interminable cattle chute-like waiting lines of the past. While there may be a wait, it is a pleasant one in which the visitor is free to explore the well-designed complex.
Photo by Author

Aerial view of the USS Arizona Memorial Visitor Center. Attractively landscaped grounds, an interior courtyard with central fountains and wide walkways, restrooms, a snack area, a well-stocked bookstore, a museum room, and twin air-conditioned theaters showing a short movie which puts the USS Arizona into the perspective of history, all combine to provide a maximum level of experience for the visitor who will soon take a shuttle boat to the memorial. **Photo Courtesy of the Arizona Memorial Museum Association**

Entrance to Visitor Center. The concrete column just right of center symbolizes the *eternal tree of life,* the same symbol found on the sides of the USS Arizona Memorial.

Photo by Author

Visitors boarding a Navy shuttle boat to make the short trip to the memorial. **Photo by Author**